COSMIC PATTERNS

COSMIC PATTERNS

a coloring book with whispers from the cosmos

Infinite Visions Publishing

Introduction

Welcome to "Cosmic Patterns - A Coloring Book with Whispers from the Cosmos." Embark on a journey unlike any other—a celestial dreamscape adventure that combines the soothing power of coloring with the cosmic energy of the universe. In these pages, you will discover a tranquil haven where swirling galaxies and intricate cosmic patterns invite you to immerse yourself in a realm of relaxation and inspiration.

As you delve into each page, you'll find more than just cosmic art to color. You'll also encounter affirmations that resonate with the stars themselves, offering you a unique opportunity to connect with the universe on a deeper level. These affirmations, like whispers from the cosmos, hold the potential to guide you toward inner harmony, clarity, and a sense of purpose.

A Celestial Dreamscape Journey:
Imagine yourself drifting through the expanse of space, surrounded by the breathtaking beauty of galaxies and cosmic wonders. As you bring life to each intricate pattern, let your mind wander among the stars, allowing the stresses of the day to gently dissolve. The act of coloring becomes a meditative practice—a way to ground yourself in the present moment and to experience the universe within you.

Affirmations from the Stars:
Each affirmation within these pages is carefully crafted to resonate with the cosmic energy that surrounds us. As you read and absorb these affirmations, you invite the wisdom of the universe to flow through you. These words are not just ink on paper; they are cosmic echoes that reflect your potential, your dreams, and your connection to the vast cosmos

A Relaxing Escape:
In a world that often moves at a rapid pace, "Cosmic Patterns" invites you to pause and take a step back. Through coloring, you can create a haven of tranquility—an oasis where time slows down, and your focus turns inward. The rhythm of your strokes and the blend of colors become a dance that mirrors the dance of the stars.

Your Personal Cosmic Journey:
This coloring book is not just a collection of patterns; it's an invitation to embark on a personal cosmic journey. As you explore each page, consider how the patterns and affirmations resonate with your own aspirations, challenges, and dreams. Allow yourself to be inspired, to reflect, and to find a sense of solace within the artistry of the cosmos.

So, open your heart and let your imagination roam as you delve into "Cosmic Patterns - A Coloring Book with Whispers from the Cosmos." May your journey through these pages be a source of relaxation, inspiration, and a reminder that you are a part of the wondrous fabric of the universe.

Let the coloring begin.

With cosmic warmth,

Infinite Visions

I am a cosmic dreamer, painting galaxies of possibility.

In the swirling cosmic patterns, I find the power to manifest my dreams.

Just as galaxies unfold, so do the layers of my inner potential.

I am a vessel of cosmic creativity, weaving dreams into existence.

My dreams dance among the stars, creating a symphony of purpose.

The universe's canvas is mine to paint with my celestial dreams.

Like swirling galaxies, my dreams spiral outward, shaping my reality.

In the cosmic tapestry, I am a unique and vibrant thread of dreams.

I am a celestial architect, crafting a dreamscape of endless wonder.

The cosmic patterns mirror the intricacies of my mind's vast potential.

My dreams are cosmic blueprints,
guiding me toward my destiny.

As stars shine, so does my inner light, guiding me to my dreams.

The galaxies whisper secrets of creation, igniting my creative spirit.

I embrace the boundless expanse of cosmic dreams within me.

The cosmic canvas reflects my dreams, each stroke a masterpiece.

In the cosmic dreamscape, I am a luminary of hope and change.

My dreams interweave with cosmic forces, shaping my journey.

Like galaxies, my dreams expand and evolve, unveiling endless horizons.

I am a conduit of cosmic inspiration, channeling dreams into reality.

The swirling galaxies mirror my thoughts, shaping my world.

With cosmic dreams, I transcend limitations and embrace possibilities.

My dreams merge with cosmic energy, fueling my journey forward.

The cosmic dance ignites my passion and lights my path to greatness.

In the embrace of cosmic patterns, my dreams take root and flourish.

The cosmos echoes my aspirations, affirming my inner strength.

I am a cosmic dream sculptor, shaping my destiny with intention.

In the midst of cosmic creation, I manifest dreams of abundance.

My dreams are cosmic beacons, guiding me through the darkness.

The swirling galaxies remind me of the boundless potential within me.

I am a cosmic dream catcher, capturing the stars of my desires.

The cosmic dreamscape is a reflection of the boundless me within.

With every breath, I inhale the energy of cosmic dreams and exhale my doubts.

Like galaxies, my dreams shimmer and dance, inspiring my journey.

I am a vessel of cosmic dreams, channeling the universe's magic.

The celestial dreamscape is my canvas, and I paint my destiny with intent.

The cosmic patterns guide me toward dreams as vast as the universe.

In the cosmic embrace, my dreams take root, becoming reality.

The swirling galaxies remind me that I am an infinite source of creation.

The cosmic dance of creation reflects my journey of self-discovery.

I am a cosmic dream alchemist, transforming intentions into reality.

I am a cosmic dream voyager, navigating the vastness of my potential.

My dreams echo in the cosmic symphony, harmonizing with the universe.

In the swirling galaxies, I find the inspiration to create my own universe.

The cosmic patterns remind me that my dreams are written in stardust.

I am a cosmic dream weaver, shaping the threads of my destiny.

Epilogue

As you close the pages of "Cosmic Patterns - A Coloring Book with Whispers from the Cosmos," you've completed more than just a coloring journey. You've embarked on a celestial odyssey, a meditative passage through swirling galaxies and intricate cosmic patterns. With each stroke of color, you've added your unique touch to the universe, creating a masterpiece that echoes the beauty of the cosmos.

But this journey goes beyond the realm of colors and lines. It's a journey into your own soul—a journey of relaxation, reflection, and discovery. Among these pages, you've found moments of tranquility that allowed you to escape the chaos of the everyday and connect with the serenity of the universe.

The affirmations that accompanied your artistic endeavors have served as guiding lights, leading you through the celestial dreamscape. They whispered secrets from the stars, reminding you of the vast potential within you, the resilience of your spirit, and the boundless creativity that resides in your heart.

As you reveled in the act of coloring, you've also experienced the magic of mindfulness. Your mind has wandered among the galaxies, and in that space between colors and shapes, you've found solace. In this sanctuary, time slowed down, and the stresses of life faded away, leaving room for peace to settle in.

Remember that this book is more than just a collection of pages; it's a companion on your journey of self-care, introspection, and growth. It's a reminder that you, like the stars that twinkle above, are an integral part of the cosmic dance. Your existence matters, and your dreams are woven into the very fabric of the universe.

As you step away from these pages, carry the serenity you've discovered with you. Allow the whispers from the cosmos to continue echoing in your heart, guiding you toward moments of calm in the midst of chaos. May the memories of this coloring journey serve as a constant reminder that the cosmos is within you, and you are a part of the cosmic tapestry.

Thank you for sharing this cosmic journey with us. May your days be filled with the same wonder and inspiration that you've found within these pages. Until we meet again under the cosmic canopy, remember that the universe always whispers its secrets to those who listen.

With cosmic gratitude,

Infinite Visions

If you liked this book please leave us a review on amazon!

Made in the USA
Monee, IL
08 October 2023

44154290R00057